A SEASON
OF REST

HOWARD BOOKS
A DIVISION OF SIMON & SCHUSTER
New York   London   Toronto   Sydney

MAL AUSTIN

picture · psaLms   *an illustrated meditation*

INTRODUCTION

"God is a never-changing God of change."

This is a quote that could be dwelt upon for quite some time and many explanations could be given, but it is perhaps the shortest and best explanation of our unchanging Lord.

We know that God's laws and decrees, as well as his attitudes and instructions on such foundations as sin and love and obedience, are eternal and unchanging. Yet we also see such tremendous differences between what the God of the Old Testament required of man versus the God of the New Testament. A new life was ushered in after Jesus' life, death, and resurrection, and the God of rules and requirements became a God of love.

To say that someone is different but hasn't changed seems contradictory. We know that change is a progression from a current state to something better or worse and that change can happen independently, around us, and not affect us. So, what is the point of change?

Change is all around us; the world and all its inhabitants are in a constant state of change; the change of seasons is just one obvious example. It seems that even though we long for warmer weather to come after winter, the beauty of the fall that welcomes in winter makes it a favorite also. There is a calming of the winds, a quietening of the forest, a yawning of the hibernating animals as preparations are made in this peaceful time for an even greater time of difference ahead.

As this photographer so loves to document the autumn, so do I realize that change is a force that cannot be avoided, a challenge that has to be faced, a movement that can be observed and marveled at; surely a gift from God.

I wonder why so many often fear change, choosing instead to view it as a negative power and stubbornly resist it. Perhaps we forget (fail?) to realize that change is of God and is so vividly portrayed physically, socially, and emotionally all around us. Jesus, Himself, called us to change, to become more like Him. He challenged us to expect great change in our walk with Him and be ready for new journeys and adventures. By His words and His actions, we are taught that we must aim to be in a constant state of growth—but it should be with His will in mind. His will for our lives is the change we should all seek.

I love to watch the forest welcome change. It doesn't resist it, as some people do; it embraces it. And because it does, the result is new life, not destruction. The very first and greatest act that takes us from the kingdom of this natural, fallen world into the supernatural kingdom of God is a decision to let Him change us. As you read these words from the Psalms and soak up the beauty of God's creation through these photographs, rest in knowing that God will not change, but will always comfort you and give you peace.

Is there then any greater thing to be had?

About the Photographer

MAL AUSTIN is one of Australia's most prominent Christian artists with a camera. A former schoolteacher, Mal now devotes his time to capturing the beauty of nature and crafting it into posters, gift cards, calendars, and books.

Eighteen years of commercial photography saw him complete over 650 weddings, and hundreds of family portraits and advertising assignments. In 2000, Mal began a new photographic direction and vision under the name of Givenworks, believing God had given him new works to do. He specializes in the use of a panoramic film camera, and his work takes him deep into the Australian and New Zealand countryside to capture many isolated places with untouched landscapes.

Mal also works in close-up floral images with an emphasis on color, pattern, shape, and texture. While some images used in this book are from large-format Pentax and Bronica film cameras, most are digitally captured using Nikon D70 and D80 cameras.

COLOR:
What a gift color is! God has blessed us with billions of colors for our use and pleasure—each as unique and special as we are. God recognizes the value of different.

LIGHT:
Any subject suddenly comes alive when a sliver of morning light hits it. Jesus is our morning light, bringing us to life, and changing us for the better.

CLOSE-UP:
God is a God of details. Look closely and you will see beauty in every feature. Don't be afraid to draw close to God. Beauty increases in closeness.

SHAPE:
Every leaf and every petal is unique by design and is then changed by weather and time, but our changes are best coming from God's Spirit.

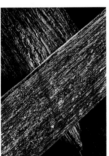

TEXTURE:
Smooth, rough, sharp, scaly; textures create interest in nature. Let time, choices, and life's experience work to form beautiful patterns in us as well.

ENVIRONMENT:
God's environment provides dew, light, sun, food, and life cycles necessary for each plant to grow. He not only meets our needs but shapes our lives in extra dimensions.

BUGS:
Even though it's often hard to see, the beauty, color, and shapes of the tiny world of bugs is around us all. God uses even the smallest of creatures for His purpose.

AGING:
Plants have a life cycle, just as we do. Each stage brings beautiful new shapes and rich, powerful colors. God loves and values life in all its glorious stages.

IN SITU:
All the images in this book were taken in their natural place of growth. We, too, grow best in the place God has chosen for us.

PSALMS 62 & 63

Finding Rest in God

I find rest in God;
only He can save me.
He is my rock and my salvation.
He is my defender;
I will not be defeated.

find rest in God

My honor and salvation
come from God.
He is my mighty rock
and my protection.
People, trust God all the time.
Tell Him all your problems,
because God is our protection.

mighty rock

God has said this,
and I have heard it over and over:
God is strong.
The Lord is loving.
You reward people
for what they have done.

The Lord is loving

God, you are my God.
I search for you.
I thirst for you like someone in a dry, empty land
where there is no water.

I search for you

I have seen you in the Temple
and have seen your strength and glory.
Because your love is better than life,
I will praise you.

better than life

I will praise you as long as I live.
I will lift up my hands
in prayer to your name.
You are my help.
Because of your protection,
I sing.

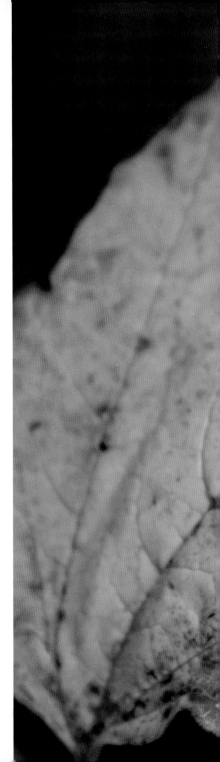

PSALM 24

Finding Peace in God

The earth is the LORD's,
and everything in it.
The world and all its people
belong to him.

For he laid the earth's foundation
on the seas
and built it on the ocean depths.

He built it

Who may climb the mountain
of the LORD?
Who may stand
in his holy place?

stand

Only those whose hands
and hearts are pure,
who do not worship idols
and never tell lies.

pure hearts

They will receive the LORD's blessing
and have a right relationship
with God their savior.

relationship

Such people may seek you
and worship in your presence,
O God of Jacob.

Open up, ancient gates!
Open up, ancient doors,
and let the King of glory enter.

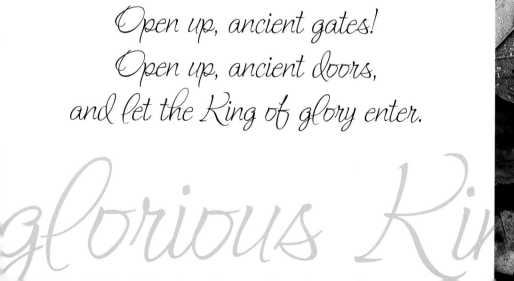

Who is the King of glory?
The LORD, strong and mighty;
the LORD, invincible in battle.

strong and might

Open up, ancient gates!
Open up, ancient doors,
and let the King of glory enter.
Who is the King of glory?
The LORD of Heaven's Armies—
he is the King of glory.

all powerful

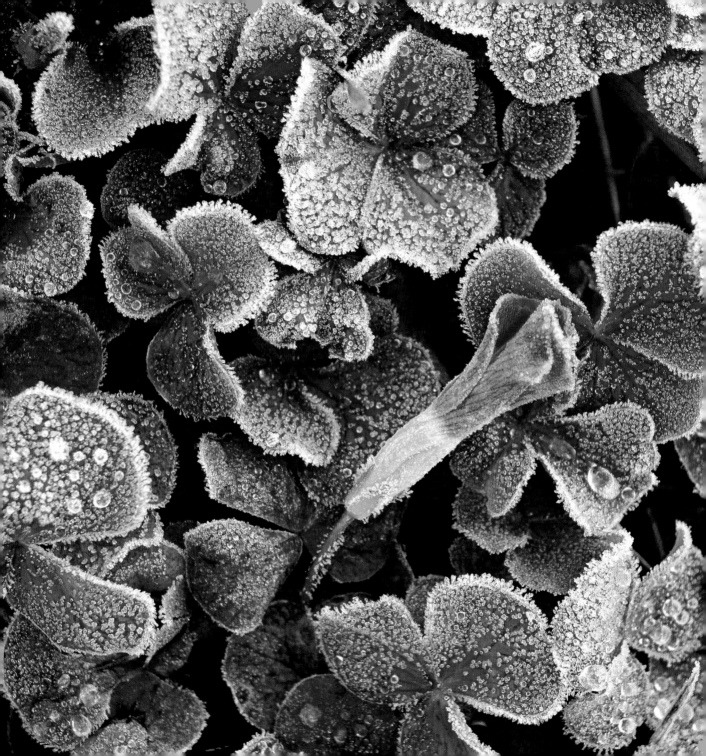

Psalm 16

Finding Hope in God

Protect me, God,
for I take refuge in You.
I said to the LORD,
"You are my Lord;
I have no good besides You." . . .

Protect me

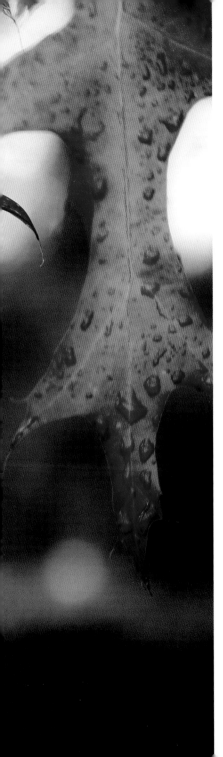

LORD, You are my portion
and my cup of blessing;
You hold my future.

The boundary lines have fallen for me
in pleasant places;
indeed, I have a beautiful inheritance.

all I need

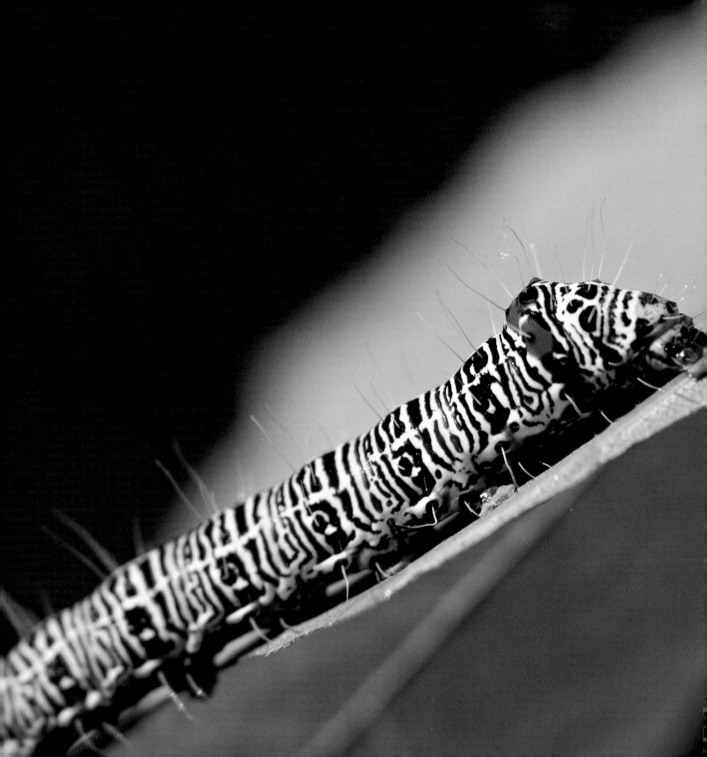

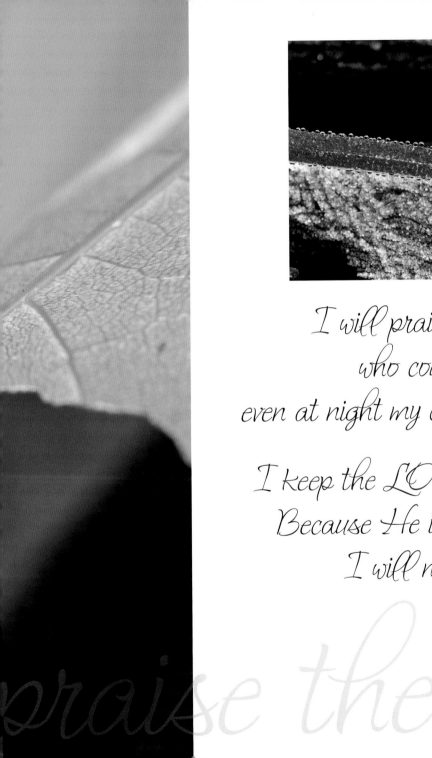

I will praise the LORD
who counsels me—
even at night my conscience instructs me.

I keep the LORD in mind always.
Because He is at my right hand,
I will not be shaken.

praise the Lord

Therefore my heart is glad,
and my spirit rejoices;
my body also rests securely. . . .

rejoice and be glad

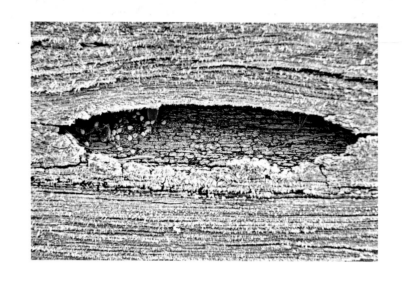

You reveal the path of life to me;
in Your presence is abundant joy;
in Your right hand are eternal pleasures.

fill me with joy

Our purpose at Howard Books is to:
• *Increase faith* in the hearts of growing Christians
• *Inspire holiness* in the lives of believers
• *Instill hope* in the hearts of struggling people everywhere
Because He's coming again!

Published by Howard Books, a Division of Simon & Schuster, Inc.
1230 Avenue of the Americas, New York, NY 10020
www.howardpublishing.com

Picture Psalms: A Season of Rest © 2007 by Mal Austin

Library of Congress Cataloging-in-Publication Data
Austin, Mal.
  A season of rest : picture Psalms : an illustrated meditation / Mal Austin.
    p. cm.
  1. Bible. O.T. Psalms—Meditations. 2. Nature—Religious aspects—Christianity. 3. Nature—Pictorial works. I. Bible. O.T. Psalms. English. Selections. 2007. II. Title.
  BS1430.54.A97 2007
  242—dc22
                                    2007018570
ISBN-13: 978-1-4165-5035-8
ISBN-10:   1-4165-5035-6
ISBN-13: 978-1-58229-709-5 (gift edition)
ISBN-10:   1-58229-709-6 (gift edition)

First Howard hardcover edition October 2007

10 9 8 7 6 5 4 3 2 1

For information regarding special discounts for bulk purchases, please contact Simon & Schuster Special Sales at 1-800-456-6798 or business@simonandschuster.com.

Edited by Chrys Howard
Cover and interior design by Stephanie D. Walker